Acknowledgements

Thank you to my wife Glenda and daughter Alicia; all of my family; Turine Tran for her beautiful illustrations; Karen at Serenity Press and everyone who shared my vision for this book. I acknowledge the traditional custodians of Australia and respect their timeless connection to this ancient and sacred land. This story is inspired by the principles of Truthfulness, Compassion and Tolerance, and dedicated to Evie and all who dream of a new world.

Foreword

Lily's journey is one that all of us take in life, rising through clouded waters until awakening to horizons that hold greater promise. May you find the courage to shine your light into the world, for yourself and others. Let the communities of humanity one day gather as flowers in a myriad of forms, each one a melody of colour unfolding with hearts in softest flame. Until the discovery of your own fire again!

Gerard Traub

Introduction

Lily the Lotus is on a very important journey, and if understood from a young age, will help guide us through life's evolutions. When a seedling is planted in healthy soil and exposed to everything it needs to thrive, it can grow into a beautiful flower for the world to behold. As a parent, I am mindful of the environment my own "seedlings" will thrive in. Gerard Traub has captured the essence of this vital component of our existence, and with the exquisite illustrations by Turine Tran, this is a book for every family to treasure.

Karen McDermott

Dedication

I am so deeply grateful to Lily. Self-knowledge requires depth and commitment to change. Lily offers us a lesson to follow her example of rising above the murky waters toward the sunshine, emerging unscathed and unblemished from her muddy pond. Touch base with your own Lily and create magic together. Happy blossoming!

Sarah Ferguson Duchess of York.

Once upon a time, in a faraway pond lived a little seed named Lily. She was quite shy, but still enjoyed playing with her friends. Lily, however, had become unhappy, as she had heard others speak of a wondrous land above the surface of the pond. It was said that in this world a magnificent light shone upon all creatures and skies of turquoise blue stretched to every horizon.

Lily longed to see the beauty of this light, but could not rise above the depths and murky waters of the pond. Her friends sometimes teased her. "There's Lily again, dreaming as usual." They told her to give up her dreams of the other world. "This is your home, Lily," they said. "Why must you seek elsewhere?" They simply could not understand her.

Even the fish swimming around her said, "Why can't you be content with who you are? We are happy here!"

Freddy, the naughtiest fish of all, roared with laughter, but Lily remained patient with him as he had recently lost his father to the line of a fisherman. She also understood that not everyone in life shares the same dream.

Lily's heart still longed for something more.

One afternoon while Lily was daydreaming, Mr Reed, known as the oldest and wisest of all in the pond, suddenly appeared. "Hello, Lily," he said.

Tears came to her eyes.

"Why are you crying?" he asked.

Lily shared her sadness with Mr Reed.

"Lily, my dear," he said, "Life is calling you to greater things, and though your eyes may not see it, your heart seeks further than the depths of your watery home. I must be on my way now, but I will speak to you again upon my return."

Soon after, Freddy rushed by and Lily could see he was quite angry. He began stirring up the mud at the bottom of the pond, making the water even murkier than usual. Suddenly, his tail became caught between two large rocks. He wriggled and splashed, yet no matter how he tried, he could not free himself. "Help!" he cried.

Lily heard his cry. She saw her friend Thomas the tortoise in the distance and called to him. "Thomas, I am so glad to see you," she said. "Freddy has caught himself between these rocks."

Thomas, a faithful friend, and a tortoise of few words, immediately got behind Freddy and pushed with all his might. Using his hard shell, he moved some of the rock until Freddy was able to break free.

"Thank you so much, Thomas," said Freddy. "If it wasn't for you and Lily, I might have been there all day."

"Don't mention it," said Thomas. "I'm always happy to lend a hand. However, I think you might owe someone an apology. You really haven't been very kind to Lily."

Thomas was right. Freddy swam over to Lily and apologised for his behaviour. "I'm so sorry, Lily. Even though I've teased you, you've never talked back to me and now you've helped to save my life. How can I ever repay you?"

Lily looked into Freddy's eyes and said, "Freddy, I've always believed you had a good heart. Can we be friends?"

"If you can ever forgive me, Lily, I would be happy to be your friend," Freddy said with a smile.

As the mud settled to the bottom of the pond, it also began to wash away from Freddy's scales. Lily could hardly believe her eyes. "Freddy, I've never seen such a splendid goldfish. You've revealed your true colours at last!"

Freddy, embarrassed now, thanked Lily and quickly said goodbye. He swam away, knowing that Lily had brought a little kindness to his heart.

Sometime later, Mr Reed returned and Lily shared with him what had happened.

He was very pleased. "Lily, because you have offered your heart to help another, you too will be granted the same opportunity."

"May I share a secret with you?" Mr Reed whispered.

"Oh yes, please do!" she cried.

"Though I might be the oldest here, I am far from the wisest. A reed can see the world above the water of the pond, and what a beautiful world it is. There are so many interesting things to see, but having lived through many seasons, I can truly say the wisest of all is the lotus flower."

Lily was surprised and looked up to his calm and gentle face. "I don't understand, Mr Reed," she said.

"You are young, Lily, but I believe it is time for you to raise yourself high, stretch yourself wide so you may blossom into whom you are destined to be."

Lily slowly lifted herself until she finally rose from the murky waters into her new world above. Lily's heart cried with joy! "At last I can see the colours of the sky, all the beauty I've seen only in my dreams."

Mr Reed could sense her joy within his own heart, too. He leaned down to Lily, and spoke. "Never again will your eyes be clouded by the waters of this pond. By the purity of your nature you have been granted the gift of a new life." Mr Reed moved a little closer and whispered, "Lily, now you have seen the land above, this world of light, but you have overlooked the most important thing of all."

Lily listened to his kind words. "Mr Reed, please tell me. I can see so many things now that I can hardly contain myself," she said.

With a soft smile he replied, "It is not what you have seen of this new world, but indeed whom you have grown into, the sweetest, most beautiful flower in the pond."

Lily turned to look at herself. She had unfolded into the splendour of a lotus flower, and as she looked further, she could see all the other lotus flowers that had raised themselves from the depths of the pond. Her longing to see beyond had finally come true.

"The beauty which has blossomed within you is also the beauty you now see all around you," said Mr Reed.

Lily at last understood, seeing the true nature of the waters below. The pond was a place where one could learn to open their own heart and mind into a land of greater things. In fact, the world above was like a reflection shining from deep inside herself. She had truly found the eyes, or rather, the heart to see a boundless sky, awakening like a new day at first light.

Lily now wanted to share her happiness with everyone living in the pond so they too could seek the beautiful world waiting to shine from within their own hearts.

The beginning...

About the Author

Lily the Lotus is Gerard Traub's first children's book composed to inspire the reader to explore the relationship between the beauty of the natural world and its deeper connection within us. He is also the author of a collection of poems entitled *Reflections of Nature*. Gerard resides with his wife and family on the Sunshine Coast, Queensland, Australia.

About the Illustrator

Turine Tran has travelled the world exploring her passion for the creative arts and storytelling. She loves to invite children and adults alike into her world of imagination where hearts can be inspired by the wonders of nature. Turine lives in Saigon, Vietnam with her two dogs.

Serenity Press Pty Ltd
Waikiki, WA 6169

First published by Serenity Press (Serenity Press Kids) in 2020
www.serenitypress.org

Copyright © Gerard Traub 2020

All rights reserved. No part of this publication may be reproduced, stored in a retrieval system, or transmitted in any form or by any means, electronic, mechanical, photocopying, recording or otherwise, without the prior written permission of the publisher.

National Library of Australia
Cataloguing in-Publication entry

Traub, Gerard (Gerard, Traub), Lily the Lotus
ISBN: 978-0-6489519-7-1 (hc)
ISBN: 978-0-6489519-6-4 (sc)
ISBN: 978-0-6489519-5-7 (e)

The National Library of Australia CIP info:
1. Juvenile fiction - general. 2. Juvenile fiction - tree. 3. Juvenile fiction - friendship

Editor: Teena Raffa-Mulligan
Copyright © Cover and illustrations by Turine Tran
Typesetting: Serenity Press Team

Printed and bound on sustainable paper in Australia

www.ingramcontent.com/pod-product-compliance
Lightning Source LLC
LaVergne TN
LVHW070612080526
838200LV00103B/346